better together*

*This book is best read together, grownup and kid.

■ akidsbookabout.com

a kids book about

DIVORCE

by Ashley Simpo

a kids book about™

Text and design copyright © 2020 by A Kids Book About, Inc.

Library of Congress Cataloging-in-Publication Data is available.

This book represents the author's personal experience and thus is not intended to be representative of every form or example of divorce as it applies to the many who have experienced it in their lives.

A Kids Book About Divorce is available online at: akidsbookabout.com

To share your stories, ask questions, or inquire about bulk purchases (schools, libraries, and non-profits), please use the following email address:

hello@akidsbookabout.com

www.akidsbookabout.com

ISBN: 9781951253271

Printed in the USA

This book is dedicated to Orion.

Thank you for always asking the hard questions,
and for being the best parts of me and your dad
all squished together.

Intro

Talking about divorce can feel incredibly awkward and even painful. It's one of those things that can't be avoided and if done wrong could have lasting effects. With all that pressure, sometimes parents are stuck searching for the right words and kids are lost in concepts far beyond their young comprehension. Things like heartbreak and joint custody feel impossible to explain.

This book will hopefully help to make this conversation a bit easier. You're not alone on this new journey, after all. Plenty of us are right here with you, and we're all going to be fine.

Hi, my name is Ashley.

I'm a writer and a mother.

I'm also **divorced**.

I have a feeling that if you're reading this book, you have questions about divorce.
Questions like.. .   .   .   .   .

WHY DO PEOPLE GET DIVORCED?

WHAT DOES DIVORCE MEAN?

If your parents are already divorced or separated, you probably have **have questions like.. . . . . .**

CAN I FIX THIS?

WHEN WILL THIS CHANGE?

DO MY PARENTS STILL

LOVE EACH OTHER?

WHAT DID I DO WRONG?

There are so many questions to ask about divorce. Fortunately, there are plenty of answers.

To better understand divorce, let's start with what marriage is.

MARRIAGE is...

an **agreement*** between two people to become a family, share a home, and love and respect each other.

*agreement means a decision you make with someone else

Marriage can last a very looooong time—

as long as those two folks
stay in agreement.

Marriages can also end.

- -

This is called **divorce**.

- -

Divorce is when two people who are married, decide to split up and no longer be a couple.

can make you feel. . . .   .   .

Like everything is
flipped upside down.

Like nothing is ever
going to be good again.

Like you don't
have a home anymore.

Like you're different
than everyone else.

Just **scared**,
lonely,
sad, or
confused.

If your parents are **divorced**,

this book is for you.

I want you to know it's

 to feel any of those feelings.

It's **O K**

to ask lots of questions and share your feelings with your parents.

And it's  to not understand why your parents got a divorce.

Now, this won't be easy,
but here are some things
you should know about divorce.

- - - - - - - - - - - - - - - - - -

First of all, your parents
will not get back together.

— — — — — — — — — — —

A divorce is not just for now,
it's for good.

Divorce means a lot of changes for everyone, and that can be **really hard**.

It can mean
a new home,
a new school,
and even
a new city.

It also means the time you spend with each parent will change.

It could be a lot of time with **one**...

and not much with **the other**.

Or spending the same
amount of time with **each**.

But you may have to go back — — —

— — — & forth between two homes.

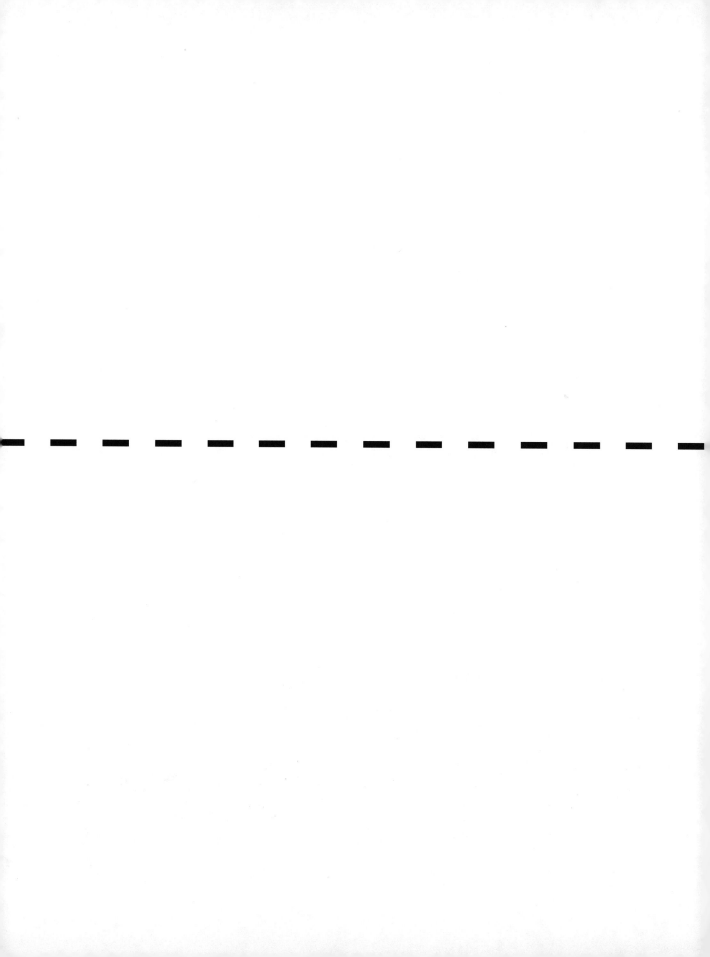

— All this change can feel **really hard**.

With all of this hard stuff, you might be wondering why your parents got a divorce at all.

Here are a few reasons
why **divorce** happens...

Some parents stop getting along.
Not over small things like...

who gets to watch TV?

but over **BIG** things like

WHAT HURTS THEM

or

WHAT MAKES THEM HAPPY.

Sometimes,

a marriage can get so broken, that no matter how hard a couple tries, they can't fix it.

Other times,
parents hurt each other.

Maybe the hurt is with words,
or maybe with hitting or pushing.

In some cases,
parents' feelings change
about each other
and they want to be alone
or with someone new.

To be honest, there are too many reasons to count why parents get a **divorce**.

Every couple is different.

Sometimes parents don't even agree on what those reasons are.

One of the things I want you to know about divorce...

is it's hard for **your parents**, too.

You might see them cry.

They might be quiet.

And sometimes they might get angry and yell.

Divorce is hard for **everyone**.

But...

That's not the end of the story.

When I got divorced,
a lot changed, but some
of the changes were good, like...

I DIDN'T HAVE TO
FEEL HURT ANYMORE.

THERE WEREN'T ANY
MORE ARGUMENTS.

AND I HAD MORE ENERGY
TO HAVE FUN
WITH MY SON!

There were some good changes
for my son too...

He got lots of happy attention
from his dad and me.

He made new traditions
with each of us, which makes
his time at each home:

SPECIAL

He got **two** bedrooms
and **two** sets of toys.

And a new family tree
with even more people on it.

His mom and his dad brought new special people into their lives who became special to him, too.

He even got new "aunts" and playmates who became like family as his parents created new lives.

Divorce makes family look like something completely

A **new** community can be brought to life out of all the pain of divorce.

This will look different at first but will one day become a part of what makes you beautiful and creative.

You might still wish your parents didn't get **divorced**.

And you might want to
find a way to fix it.

But, I want you to know
your parents' divorce is
NOT about you.

You didn't make it happen, and you can't make it unhappen.

And that's

You still get to be you,
and will still be the most
important part of your family.

And your parents will always
be your family,

even if
your
family
looks
different
now.

Outro

That wasn't so bad was it?

Now is a great time for some reassuring hugs and checking in with how everyone feels. This is also a good time to ask more questions.

What changes will be coming next?

Will there be any new people coming into our lives? Who are the important people that make up our community?

What traditions can we create as things change?

What will holidays and vacations be like now?

Even if there are no questions right now, questions may come later. The door to talk stays open and no question is too big or small.

find more kids books about

bullying, disabilities, empathy, creativity, racism, shame, adventure, belonging, failure, money, and anxiety.

■ **akidsbookabout.com**

share your read*

*Tell somebody, post a photo, or give this book away to share what you care about.

@akidsbookabout